THE
EDGE OF GLORY

THE
EDGE OF GLORY
Prayers in the Celtic Tradition

David Adam

MOREHOUSE PUBLISHING

First published in Great Britain 1985
Triangle/SPCK

Published in the United States of America by
Morehouse Publishisng
PO Box 1321
Harrisburg, PA 17105

Morehouse'Publishing is a divison of The Morehouse Group.

Acknowledgements

The prayer 'Deep peace of the running wave…' is reproduced by permission of the Iona Community.

The prayer 'Christ be near…' is a translation of St. Patrick's Breastplate
from *The People's Mass Book* by J. Fennelly, published by Gill & Macmil-
lan Ltd. Used by permission.

Cover design by Corey R. Kent.

Library of Congress Cataloging-in-Publication Data
Adam, David.
  The edge of glory.

  Reprint. Originally published: London: Triangle, © 1985.
  1. Prayers.   I. Title
BV245.A3   1988   242'.8'0089916   87-31227

ISBN: 0-8192-1418-3

Printed in the United States of America

03 02 01 00 99 98   10 9 8 7 6 5 4

TO DENISE AND JANE
for loving and supporting
two scribes from the Dark Ages

ACKNOWLEDGEMENTS

I should like to thank Peter Dingle for the majority of drawings in this book; may he continue to weave the mysteries. To the other artists, Anne Gilbert, Elisabeth Randles and Jenny Pearson I am extremely grateful. All are members of the parish where this book originated.

Without John Harwood's enthusiasm and encouragement, and Sharon Artley's typing, this work would never have been completed.

As always I am thankful for such an understanding and loving wife. To Denise for her willingness to make constant pilgrimages to Anglo-Saxon and Celtic holy places.

Contents

FOREWORD by Bishop Stuart Blanch *ix*

INTRODUCTION *1*

1 BEFORE PRAYER *5*

2 THROUGH THE DAY *17*

3 BENEDICTIONS *47*

4 FOR GROUP WORSHIP *59*

5 ANCIENT AND TRADITIONAL PRAYERS *83*

6 ST PATRICK'S BREASTPLATE *97*

7 THOUGHTS ON HOLY ISLAND *107*

Foreword

by Bishop Stuart Blanch

David Adam was known to me throughout my time as Archbishop of York, and I well remember the ordination retreat that he took for us at Bishopthorpe. He was regarded as a conscientious and imaginative parish priest, at home in the country and amongst country people. But his reputation did not then include the literary art which is so evident in this book. However, he would be the first to admit that this book is not the product of a single mind, but of a group of like-minded people meeting over a long period to try to discover new springs of spiritual life, new forms of prayer, and a new understanding of the gospel. I commend it whole-heartedly to the reader, not only for its attractive format and evocative style, but for the new insights it offers into the faith of our northern forefathers who did so much to shape the religion of this land. Their faith awaits a revival in our somewhat tired, over-formalized, despairing society.

The book could be used with profit by individuals, by study groups and by congregations in the normal worship of the Church. It is a book of joyful prayer wrought out of the stuff of everyday life, and contributing richly to it. David and his friends and his illustrators are to be congratulated on the fruits of what he has called 'a journey of discovery'.

Introduction

Whoever wrote St Patrick's Breastplate, has certainly caught the essence of Celtic prayer.

Patrick, arising in the morning and turning his thoughts to God, taking to himself the whole armour of God. As he laced up his tunic or the crossbands on his legs, he had his dressing prayer.

> I bind unto myself today
> The strong name of the Trinity,
> By invocation of the same,
> The Three in One and One in Three.

Beginning the day, expressing belief in and calling upon the Sacred Three. Going on to contemplate the life of Christ:

> I bind this day to me for ever,
> By power of faith, Christ's incarnation;
> His baptism in the Jordan river;
> His death on cross for my salvation.

Not just a God of history, but a God who is very near and at all times ready to give a hand if we call upon him:

> I bind unto myself today
> The power of God to hold and lead,
> His eye to watch, his might to stay,
> His ear to hearken to my need.

A God ever present, ready to save and heal, especially in the Incarnate Lord.

St Patrick would very much agree with Angelus Silesius who wrote:

> Though Christ a thousand times
> In Bethlehem be born
> If he's not born in thee
> Thy soul is still forlorn.
>
> The cross on Golgotha
> Will never save thy soul.
> The cross in thine own heart
> Alone can make thee whole.

The history of salvation and incarnation has to become our own personal history. The Celtic way of ever inviting God into their activities and seeking to become aware of him in everyday events is the most natural way of achieving this. The last verse of St Patrick's hymn is worth a daily meditation:

> Christ be with me, Christ within me,
> Christ behind me, Christ before me,
> Christ beside me, Christ to win me,
> Christ to comfort and restore me,
> Christ beneath me, Christ above me,
> Christ in quiet, Christ in danger,
> Christ in hearts of all that love me,
> Christ in mouth of friend and stranger.

Here we have a weaving of the Presence around our lives like the Celtic patterns on stones and in the illuminated Gospels: Christ moves in and out, over and under. We are encircled by him; encompassed by his presence and love.

This is not something we create, it is a reality to become aware of, a glory that is ours but that we so often miss. We are on the very edge of glory, but we seem to choose the wrong side.

When St Aidan died, Cuthbert had a vision of him being lifted up to heaven and he said:

'What wretches we are, given up to sleep and sloth so that we never see the glory of those who watch with Christ unceasingly. After so short a vigil what marvels I have seen.'

The prayers in this book are written out of a desire to walk the edge of glory and see for oneself the ever abiding presence, that never leaves us or forsakes us: the encompassing God, the watchful eye, the strong helping hand, the power of the Spirit. Only then can we go out in mission, for then we go not in our own strength and ideas, but in the power and love of the God who abides.

If prayer has become boring, or you have ceased to pray, there is nothing wrong with prayer — and the Almighty cannot be boring. There is something wrong with the way you are doing it. Too much of prayer has lost its rhythm — seek to find it. Prayer that has lost its simplicity of relationship with God is too contrived . . . above all things, seek him. If there is to be any real glory in your life, remember it is his and from him. See if you can step over the edge of glory — as the spiritual says:

> Oh you gotta get a glory
> In the work you do,
> A Halleluiah chorus
> In the heart of you.
> Paint or tell a story,
> Sing or shovel coal,
> But you gotta get a glory
> Or the job lacks soul.

1

BEFORE PRAYER

Before Prayer

I weave a silence on to my lips
I weave a silence into my mind
I weave a silence within my heart
I close my ears to distractions
I close my eyes to attractions
I close my heart to temptations

Calm me O Lord as you stilled the storm
Still me O Lord, keep me from harm
Let all the tumult within me cease
Enfold me Lord in your peace

Circle me Lord
Keep protection near
And danger afar

Circle me Lord
Keep hope within
Keep doubt without

Circle me Lord
Keep light near
And darkness afar

Circle me Lord
Keep peace within
Keep evil out

The Trinity

The Trinity
Protecting me
The Father be
Over me
The Saviour be
Under me
The Spirit be
About me
The Holy Three
Defending me
As evening come
Bless my home
Holy Three
Watching me
As shadows fall
Hear my call
Sacred Three
Encircle me
So it may be
Amen to Thee
Holy Three
About me

The Eternal

As He is
He was:
As He was
He is.
He shall be
As He is
And was
The eternal
Forever
So be it
Amen
The forever
Eternal
So be it
Amen

Adoration

I bow before the Father
Who made me
I bow before the Son
Who saved me
I bow before the Spirit
Who guides me
In love and adoration
I give my lips
I give my heart
I give my mind
I give my strength
I bow and adore thee
Sacred Three
The Ever One
The Trinity

Thanksgiving

Thanks be to thee, for the gifts thou givest me
Each day, each night, on land and sea
Each weather, fair, wild or calm
For thine eye to keep from harm
For each hour, its ebb, its flow
For thine arm around me so
For each gift thanks be to thee
The best gift is thyself to me

Thou Art God

Thou art the peace of all things calm
Thou art the place to hide from harm
Thou art the light that shines in dark
Thou art the heart's eternal spark
Thou art the door that's open wide
Thou art the guest who waits inside
Thou art the stranger at the door
Thou art the calling of the poor
Thou art my Lord and with me still
Thou art my love, keep me from ill
Thou art the light, the truth, the way
Thou art my Saviour this very day.

All that I am I give you Lord
All that I am I give you

All that I have I share with you Lord
All that I have I share with you

All my life is yours Lord
All my life is yours

All my desires are yours Lord
All my desires are yours

All my hopes are in you Lord
All my hopes are in you

All I want is you Lord
All I want is you

Inspired by the marriage service.
Best said by two people or a single person and
a group.

2

———

THROUGH THE DAY

New Day

This new day you give to me
From your great eternity
This new day now enfold
Me in your loving hold

You are the star of the morn
You are the day newly born
You are the light of our night
You are the Saviour by your might

God be in me this day
God ever with me stay
God be in the night
Keep us by thy light
God be in my heart
God abide, never depart.

Each Day

God be supervising
My sleeping and my rising
God be with me waking
Bless each undertaking
God's almighty powers
Keep my daylight hours
God's Spirit strengthen
My days as they lengthen

Dedication

I give my hands to you Lord
I give my hands to you

I offer the work I do Lord
I offer the work I do

I give my thoughts to you Lord
I give my thoughts to you

I give my plans to you Lord
I give my plans to you

Give your hands to me Lord
Give your hands to me

Let your love set me free Lord
Let your love set me free

Keep me close to you Lord
Keep me close to you.

Give to me O God
A clear and watchful eye

Give to me O God
A firm but gentle touch

Give to me O God
A good receptive ear

Give to me O God
A clean discerning taste

Give to me O God
A subtle sense of smell

Give to me O God
An openness to others

Give to me O God
An awareness now of you.

Give me O God
Each thing that is needful for my body.

Give me O God
That which will renew my mind.

Give me O God
That which will strengthen my spirit.

Give me O God
Healing for my sickness.

Give me O God
Repentance for my sin.

Give to me O God
Yourself above all else.

Opening of the Senses

Blessings today, God, give unto me
Blessings today in all that I see

Blessings today, God, draw near
Blessings today in all that I hear

Blessings today, God, let them be such
Blessings today in all that I touch

Blessings today, God, and joy as well
Blessings today in all that I smell

Blessings today, God, let nothing waste
Blessings today in all that I taste

Blessings today, God, in meeting another
Blessings today, you come as my brother

Blessings today, God, in all I discover
Blessings today, you come as my lover

Blessings today, God, make me aware
Blessings today, for you are there.

An Oblation

I place my hands in yours Lord
I place my hands in yours

I place my will in yours Lord
I place my will in yours

I place my days in yours Lord
I place my days in yours

I place my thoughts in yours Lord
I place my thoughts in yours

I place my heart in yours Lord
I place my heart in yours

I place my life in yours Lord
I place my life in yours

Incarnatus Est

Glory to God on earth peace
Let this song never cease.

As I arise this morn
Christ in me be born

When I wash my face
Bless me with your grace

When I comb my hair
Keep me from despair

When I put on my clothes
Your presence Lord disclose

This is the day that you are born
Let every day be a Christmas morn

Glory to God on earth peace
Let this song never cease.

The sacred Three be over me
With my working hands this day
With the people on my way
With the labour and the toil
With the land and with the soil
With the tools that I take
With the things that I make
With the thoughts of my mind
With the sharing with mankind
With the love of my heart
With each one who plays a part
The sacred Three be over me
The blessing of the Trinity.

At Fire Lighting

As I light this fire Lord
I bend my knee and lay myself before you.
Kindle in my heart a flame of love
Love to warm my home and all my dear ones
Love to cheer my neighbours and this community.
Love to comfort my friend and foe
Love to lighten the way I go.
Lord, as I light this fire
I lay myself before you.

Lord be a bright flame before me
Be a guiding light above me
Be a warm welcome ahead of me
Today, tomorrow and forever.

Breaking New Land

All that I dig with the spade
I do it with my Father's aid

All that I dig with the spade
I do it with my Saviour's aid

All that I dig with the spade
I do it with the Spirit's aid

All that I dig with the spade
I do it in God the Three's aid.
Each turning of the soil I make
I do it for the Three in One's sake.

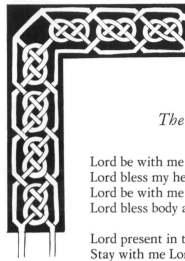

The Real Presence

Lord be with me in the breaking of the bread
Lord bless my heart, my hands, my head
Lord be with me offering the wine
Lord bless body and soul, they are thine

Lord present in the wine and bread
Stay with me Lord when I am fed
Bless the way by which I go
Guide me in this world below

Lord thou art there in bread and wine
Around my life may thou entwine
Bless O Lord the life I lead
From sin and stain keep me freed

Thy Presence come between me
And all things evil
Thy Presence come between me
And all things vile
Thy Presence come between me
And all things of guile
Thy Presence come between me
And all things that defile
Keep me O Lord as the apple of thine eye
Hide me under the shadow of thy wings.

Journeying

I set my little ship to sea
Let thine eye Lord be over me
My little craft upon the brine
Keep me Lord for I am thine

This day dear Lord with me go
If life ebb or if it flow
This day dear Lord be with me
On firm ground or all at sea

God ahead, God behind
God be on the path I wind
God above, God below
God be everywhere I go
God in the steep
God in the shade
God me safe keep
Come to my aid.

On ocean deep
Keep me Saviour keep
As I go over land
Give me thy hand
When troubles come nigh
Protect with thine eye
From all that I dread
Lord may I be led

Lord, the sea is so large
And my boat is so small

Prayer of the Breton fishermen

Christmas Poor

You are the caller
You are the poor
You are the stranger at my door

You are the wanderer
The unfed
You are the homeless
With no bed

You are the man
Driven insane
You are the child
Crying in pain

You are the other who comes to me
If I open to another you're born in me

Lord Lift Me

Lord from this world's stormy sea
Give your hand for lifting me
Lord lift me from the darkest night
Lord lift me into the realm of light
Lord lift me from this body's pain
Lord lift me up and keep me sane
Lord lift me from the things I dread
Lord lift me from the living dead
Lord lift me from the place I lie
Lord lift me that I never die.

I Bind Unto Myself Today

By the rowan and the briar
By the raging forest fire
By the sky in lightning torn
By the moon that's newly born
By the rising of the sun
By the task that I have done
I bind my feeble soul to thee
Almighty, Son and Spirit Three.

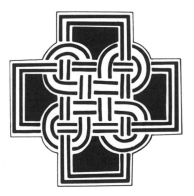

Good Shepherd

> be over me to shelter me
> under me to uphold me
> behind me to direct me
> before me to lead me
> about me to protect me
> ever with me to save me
> above me to lift me

and bring me to the green pasture of eternal life.

Night Prayers

As I enter into sleep
Keep me Father keep
As I seek a safe repose
Christ my eyelids close
As I take my rest
Spirit keep me with the blest
Holy Blessed Three
Keep me close to Thee
That refreshed I may wake
To work again for thy sake

God in the night
God at my right
God all the day
God with me stay
God in my heart
Never depart
God with thy might
Keep us in light
Through this dark night

My body soul and mind
Thy sanctuary will find
In that holy place
Keep me by thy grace
Let sleep come upon me
With the covering of the Three.
Father watch with thine eye
Saviour keep me lest I die
Spirit stay ever nigh
My sleep safe will be
Through the Holy Trinity.

O God of light, God of might
Keep me ever in your sight
Grant my eyes to safely sleep
While you dear Lord my soul shall keep

Come Holy Dove

When I feel alone
Your presence is ever with me.
Come Holy Dove
Cover with love

When I am in the dark
Your light is all around me.
Come Holy Dove
Cover with love

When I am in the cold
Your warmth will enfold me.
Come Holy Dove
Cover with love

When I feel weak
Your strength will seek me.
Come Holy Dove
Cover with love

When I am sad
Your joy will make me glad.
Come Holy Dove
Cover with love

When I am sick and ill
Your health will heal me still.
Come Holy Dove
Cover with love

Spirit be about my head
Spirit peace around me shed
Spirit light about my way
Spirit guardian night and day

Come Holy Dove
Cover with love

Jesus be there at the start
Jesus remain in my heart
Jesus be there in the fight
Jesus be there with your might
Jesus be there as a friend
Jesus be there to the end

Saviour of my soul
This day keep me whole
All the long day light
And through the darkness of the night

The Conqueror

Lord strengthen every good
Defeat the power of evil

Lord strengthen every light
Defeat the power of darkness

Lord strengthen every power
Defeat the power of weakness

Lord strengthen every joy
Defeat the power of sadness

Lord strengthen every love
Defeat the power of hatred

Lord strengthen every life
Defeat the power of death

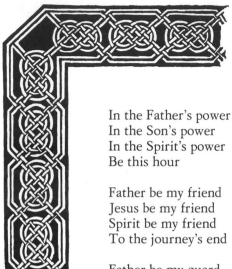

In the Father's power
In the Son's power
In the Spirit's power
Be this hour

Father be my friend
Jesus be my friend
Spirit be my friend
To the journey's end

Father be my guard
Jesus be my guard
Spirit be my guard
When the way is hard

In the Father's power
In the Son's power
In the Spirit's power
Be this hour

The Father who created me
With thine eye watch me
Saviour who redeemed me
With thine eye look on me
Spirit who strengthens me
With thine eye regard me
The eyeing of the Three
For my saving be

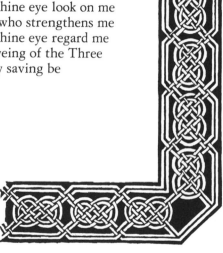

3

BENEDICTIONS

A Weaving Pattern

The weaving of peace be thine
Peace around thy soul entwine
Peace of the Father flowing free
Peace of the Son sitting over thee
Peace of the Spirit for thee and me
Peace of the one
Peace of the Three
A weaving of peace be upon thee

Around thee twine the Three
The One the Trinity
The Father bind his love
The Son tie his salvation
The Spirit wrap his power
Make you a new creation
Around thee twine the Three
The encircling of the Trinity

Encircling

The circle of Jesus keep you from sorrow
The circle of Jesus today and tomorrow
The circle of Jesus your foes confound
The circle of Jesus your life surround

The Father on you his blessing bestow
The Son his love towards you flow
The Spirit his presence to you show
On you and all the folk you know
On you and all who around you go
The Threefold blessing may you know

The joy of this day be yours
The joy of this week be yours
The joy of this year be yours
The joy of the Father be yours
The joy of the Spirit be yours
The joy of the Son be yours
Joy for ever and ever be yours

The hands of the Father uphold you
The hands of the Saviour enfold you
The hands of the Spirit surround you
And the blessing of God Almighty
Father, Son and Holy Spirit
Uphold you evermore. Amen

Journeying

The Lord be with your going
Bless you in your coming
The Presence be with your travels
Bless the road as it unravels

God go with thee on the road
Go thou out in the power of God
God go with thee on thy way
God protect thee from the fray
God keep thy body and thy soul
God watch thee as the years roll

God keep you safe when the cliffs are sheer
God keep you safe when the night is drear
God keep you safe on the path you tread
God keep you and be with you at your head

House Blessings

God give grace
To this dwelling place

Christ give grace
To this dwelling place

Spirit give grace
To this dwelling place

Bless the father of this house
Bless the father and his spouse
Bless the children growing tall
Bless the family one and all

Peace be upon all within
Peace to keep you free from sin
Peace upon your neighbours all
Peace be upon those who call

God bless this house from roof to floor
God bless the windows and the door
God bless us all evermore
God bless the house with fire and light
God bless each room with thy might
God with thy hand keep us right
God be with us in this dwelling site

The Father is in the house
Nothing need we fear

Christ is in the house
Loving us so dear

The Spirit is in the house
Listening to our prayer

The Three are in the house
Always very near

Peace be in my life
Peace be to my wife
Peace be to my children small
Peace be on all who call
Peace of the Father be mine
Peace of the Saviour entwine
Peace of the Spirit enthrall
Peace of the Three be on all

The Good Shepherd

The herding of the shepherd
Keep you safe from danger
Free you from harm

The herding of the shepherd
Keep you safe from sickness
Free you from alarm

The herding of the shepherd
Keep you from despair
Have you in his care

The herding of the shepherd
Keep you from sorrow
Today and tomorrow

The shepherd's love enfold
Keep you in his hold

The shepherd's might enclasp
Keep you in his grasp

Christ our Shepherd King
Our praises to thee we sing

Easter Blessing

The Lord of the empty tomb
The conqueror of gloom
Come to you

The Lord in the garden walking
The Lord to Mary talking
Come to you

The Lord in the Upper Room
Dispelling fear and doom
Come to you

The Lord on the road to Emmaus
The Lord giving hope to Thomas
Come to you

The Lord appearing on the shore
Giving us life for ever more
Come to you

4

FOR GROUP WORSHIP

Many of the prayers in this book began in a small room in a moorland village in 1984. They were part of our Lent learning: for six weeks we met once a week to discover new and exciting ways of praying together. As we live in an area famous for its Celtic saints and Anglo-Saxon spirituality, we looked for early patterns of prayer. We had the 'Song of Caedmon', but it was hard to find really early models. So we turned to the prayers from the Hebrides as found in *Poems of the Western Highlanders* by G.R.D. McLean (SPCK 1961).

Ours was to be a journey of discovery; we sought prayers that would vibrate with the presence of God. We said that prayer should be thrilling, that once again it should be something we wanted to do. There seemed so much *gravitas* over-burdening many of our prayers — prayer should at least be joyful, if not fun. We prayed with St Teresa, 'Lord, deliver us from sour-faced saints.' Some of us spent a few days on Lindisfarne learning of Aidan and Cuthbert, others visited Bede's monastery at Jarrow and Cuthbert's shrine at Durham; one group went to Whithorn and returned to tell us of St Ninian. We were in no doubt that it was prayer that strengthened these saints and made them joyful.

We firmly believed in the Incarnation, so we sought a new earthiness in our prayers. They were to be truly grounded, they related to the lives we lived. As a passing thought, we decided that humility and humus were closely linked. Unless our prayers were at home in our home and our garden, they were probably not at home anywhere. We wanted prayers we could use as we moved about. Our journey became a pilgrimage; we sought each day to move nearer to God in our thoughts and actions. We sought to step over the Edge of Glory.

Too much of what is called public prayer is one person performing and the others being passive. We wanted greater involvement, for more people to make their own personal contribution. As a base for such experiments we used the Creed Prayer that Alexander Carmichael was taught by the crofter Mary Gillies of Morar. In this book the prayer *Affirmation* is based on the Creed Prayer. We found this a very exciting prayer to use. We used it in church, at Sunday school, at retreats, at camp fire services and in day school: everywhere it was met with enthusiasm. A leader would say the first line, 'I believe O God of all gods that you are . . .' so affirming the Eternal Presence — then after two beats of a drum or tambourine, someone would say 'The eternal Father of . . .' adding an attribute of God they wanted to declare. Then another two drumbeats, and the leader would start again, and so on. In some groups it was possible to talk about why we had declared that God had whatever we personally attributed to him. Similar use can be made of the prayer, *Your Presence Lord:* this time the leader saying the first sentence, a group the second, and an individual the third.

Many of the prayers to the Trinity are for three voices or groups. The simplest of these is *The Blessing of the Flocks:* its refrains, 'Father bless . . . Jesus bless . . . Spirit bless' are easy for even the youngest to follow. In this type of prayer the leadership can move around to anyone who wants to ask God's blessing on someone or something. We have used it on the theme of mines, or boats and fishermen, or homes and schools; the list could be endless. Prayers that are also in this way of praying are: *A Threefold Prayer, Father when we are troubled, Creator help us,* and *In the Father's power* (Section 2). Other prayers can be used antiphonally, for two voices or the leader and a group. Among these are *All that I am I give you* (Section 1), *An Oblation* (Section 2), *All My Longings, Dedication.* In these prayers it is still possible for people to add verses at will.

Prayers like *Opening Prayer, Maranatha, Come Holy Dove* (Section 2) and *The Love of God* are prayers for a leader and a chorus: they are also very effective with just the use of two voices. All the prayers in this section are meant as basic prayers to guide people and help them make their own experiments in prayer.

What a joy it is when a group finds a common purpose and works with enthusiasm. It is when we are enthused that we really achieve things: the very word 'enthuse' means being in God. So our little group that met together in Lent 1984 enthused as we discovered, for us, new ways of prayer. What we now ask of God is that our experiments, prayers and drawings will encourage others to walk the Edge of Glory. May you discover the pathway that leads into the Presence.

P. Dingle.

Opening Prayer

God be with us
Amen
The Lord be with you
And with your spirit too

The Father be with us
Amen
The Creator be with you
And with your spirit too

Jesus be with us
Amen
The Saviour be with you
And with your spirit too

The Spirit be with us
Amen
The Strengthener be with you
And with your spirit too

The Trinity be with us
Amen
The Sacred Three be over you
And with your spirit too

God be with us
Amen

Affirmations

I believe O God of all gods that you are
The Eternal Father of Life

I believe O God of all gods that you are
The Eternal Father of Love

I believe O God of all gods that you are
The Eternal Father of Peace

I believe O God of all gods that you are
The Eternal Father of Joy

I believe O God of all gods that you are
The Eternal Father of the saints

I believe O God of all gods that you are
The Eternal Father the Creator

I believe O God of all gods that you are
The Eternal Father strong to save

I believe O God of all gods that you are
The Eternal Father of me.

Creator help us to hear
Saviour help us to hear
Sanctifier help us to hear

Creator help us to see
Saviour help us to see
Sanctifier help us to see

Creator help us to be aware
Saviour help us to be aware
Sanctifier help us to be aware

Creator help us to care
Saviour help us to care
Sanctifier help us to care

Creator sharpen our senses
Saviour sharpen our senses
Sanctifier sharpen our senses

A Threefold Prayer

Father in heaven hear us
Jesus our Saviour hear us
Spirit our Strengthener hear us

Father in heaven guide us
Jesus our Saviour guide us
Spirit our Strengthener guide us

Father in heaven help us
Jesus our Saviour help us
Spirit our Strengthener help us

Father in heaven we love you
Jesus our Saviour we love you
Spirit our Strengthener we love you

Father in heaven we need you
Jesus our Saviour we need you
Spirit our Strengthener we need you

Father in heaven come to us
Jesus our Saviour come to us
Spirit our Strengthener come to us

Father when we are troubled calm us
Jesus when we are troubled calm us
Spirit when we are troubled calm us

Father when we are weary rest us
Jesus when we are weary rest us
Spirit when we are weary rest us

Father when we are angry settle us
Jesus when we are angry settle us
Spirit when we are angry settle us

Father when we are in danger protect us
Jesus when we are in danger protect us
Spirit when we are in danger protect us

Father when we are warring pacify us
Jesus when we are warring pacify us
Spirit when we are warring pacify us

If there is a leader, he or she may end
with a request to the Sacred Three:

> Three in One, One in Three
> Give us peace evermore.

All My Longings

My life cries out for you Lord
My life cries out for you

My love seeks out for you Lord
My love seeks out for you

My heart yearns for you Lord
My heart yearns for you

My mind thinks of you Lord
My mind thinks of you

My strength strives for you Lord
My strength strives for you

Dedication

I give myself to you Lord
I give myself to you

With my mind and its thinking
I give myself to you

With my hands and their working
I give myself to you

With my eyes and their seeing
I give myself to you

With my body and its actions
I give myself to you

With my heart and its loving
I give myself to you

I give myself to you Lord
I give myself to you

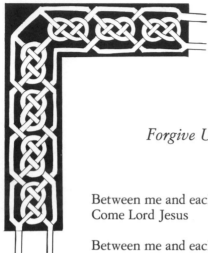

Forgive Us Lord

Between me and each evil deed
Come Lord Jesus

Between me and each sinful act
Come Lord Jesus

Between me and each wicked thought
Come Lord Jesus

Between me and each wrong desire
Come Lord Jesus

The Cross between me and all ill
The Cross to foil the devil's skill

The Cross between me and all harm
The Cross to foil all evil's charm

Jesus Saviour of us all
Give us forgiveness as we call
Help us forget the evil past
Give us a hope that will last
From wicked ways may we abstain
Avoid the deeds that give Thee pain.

Christ in forgiveness to me be near
Christ in forgiveness come appear
Christ in forgiveness drive off the foe
Christ in forgiveness help me below
Christ in forgiveness give me release
Christ in forgiveness I need thy peace

For Aid

We bring (*name*) in weakness
For your strengthening

We bring (*name*) in sickness
For your healing

We bring (*name*) in trouble
For your calming

We bring (*name*) who is lost
For your guidance

We bring (*name*) who is lonely
For your love

We bring (*name*) who is dying
For your resurrection.

Father us surround
Every foe confound

Jesus entwine
Keep us thine

Spirit enfold
In thy hold

Sacred three enthrall
To thee we call

Father
Create this day without sorrow
Create us hope for the morrow

Jesus in thy hands grasping
Lift us to life everlasting

Spirit fill us with love
That our lives shall improve

Holy blessed three
We are ever with thee.

Total Immersion

Water baptism is not enough; we must totally
immerse ourselves, our children and our world
in the Sacred Three. Before each verse, we
could speak the name of a godchild or loved one.

In the presence of the Father I immerse thee
That to thee he may protecting be
Watching over thy head
Keeping thee from dread
In the presence of the Creator I immerse thee.

In the presence of the Son I immerse thee
That to thee He may a Saviour be
May He keep thee whole and well
Save thee from the jaws of hell
In the presence of the Redeemer I immerse thee.

In the presence of the Spirit I immerse thee
That He may a mighty strengthener be
May He guide thee, lead, empower
Give thee hope in the darkest hour
In the Spirit the life-giver I immerse thee.

In the Holy and blessed Three, I immerse thee
Into their love and joy I place thee
Into their peace and power I steep thee
Into the hands that will keep thee
Into the Trinity of love I immerse thee.

We beseech Thee O God open thy heavens.
From there may thy gifts descend upon *him*.
Put forth thine own hand from heaven and
    touch *his* head.
May *he* feel the touch of thine hand and
    receive the joy
of thy Holy Spirit. That *he* may
    remain blessed for evermore.

St Ethelwold   *925*

Your Presence Lord

You Lord are in the world
Your Presence fills it
Your Presence is PEACE

You Lord are in this place
Your Presence fills it
Your Presence is PEACE

You Lord are in my life
Your Presence fills it
Your Presence is PEACE

You Lord are in my heart
Your Presence fills it
Your Presence is PEACE.

Use this prayer every day only changing what you want to declare about the Lords' Presence. A suggested pattern is as follows:

Sunday	PEACE
Monday	JOY
Tuesday	FAITH
Wednesday	HOPE
Thursday	LOVE
Friday	GLORY
Saturday	LIFE

A Simple Blessing of the Flocks

Father bless the lambs
Jesus bless the lambs
Spirit bless the lambs

Father bless the ewes
Jesus bless the ewes
Spirit bless the ewes

Father bless the rams
Jesus bless the rams
Spirit bless the rams

Father bless the farms
Jesus bless the farms
Spirit bless the farms

Father bless the land
Jesus bless the land
Spirit bless the land

Father bless our lives
Jesus bless our lives
Spirit bless our lives

Used on Good Shepherd Sunday when the lambs are
brought to church to be blessed.
Similar prayers are used at Rogation time: it is
just as easy to have a prayer for the blessing of
the fleet or for the blessing of the mine or factory,
and more powerful if used in the place prayed for.

The Love of God

What can separate us from the love of God?
Can sickness or death?
No nothing can separate us from the love of God

Can danger or war?
No nothing can separate us from the love of God

Can sadness or despair?
No nothing can separate us from the love of God

Can the nuclear bomb or the end of the world?
No nothing can separate us from the love of God

Can failure or rejection?
No nothing can separate us from the love of God

Can loneliness or fear?
No nothing can separate us from the love of God

The Power of God

Lord all power is yours
The power of the atom is yours
The power of the spacecraft is yours
The power of the computer is yours
The power of the jet is yours
The power of the television is yours
The power of electricity is yours
Lord all power is yours
On loan it is ours
Lord let us use it aright
That it reveal your might
Lord all power is yours

God of Space

Lord you are the star ranger
Yet to us you are no stranger

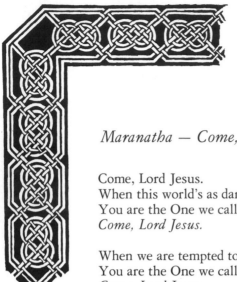

Maranatha — Come, Lord Jesus

Come, Lord Jesus.
When this world's as dark as night
You are the One we call the light.
Come, Lord Jesus.

When we are tempted to go astray
You are the One we call the way.
Come, Lord Jesus.

When we are falling in the strife
You are the One who is the life.
Come, Lord Jesus.

When troubles to our lives bring harm
You are the One who brings us calm.
Come, Lord Jesus.

When the storms of life increase
You are the One who is our peace.
Come, Lord Jesus.

When our lives are full of woe
You are the One to whom we go.
Come, Lord Jesus.

When we are down and all forlorn
Come as the resurrection morn.
Come, Lord Jesus.

When our lives are full of sin
You are the One who death does win.
Come, Lord Jesus.

5

ANCIENT AND
TRADITIONAL PRAYERS

For God's Safe Keeping

May the strength of God pilot us.
May the power of God preserve us.
May the wisdom of God instruct us.
May the hand of God protect us.
May the way of God direct us.
May the shield of God defend us.
May the host of God guard us
against the snares of the evil one
And the temptations of the world.
May Christ be with us
Christ above us
Christ in us
Christ before us.
May thy salvation O Lord,
Be always ours
This day and for evermore

                                    Amen

                    St Patrick   373

The Song of Caedmon

Now must we praise the Warden of Heaven's realm
The Creator's might and his mind's thought,
The glorious works of the Father;
How of every wonder
He, the Lord, the eternal, laid the foundation.
He shaped erst, for the sons of men,
Heaven as their roof, Holy Creator,
The middle-world, He, mankind's Warden,
Eternal Lord, afterwards prepared
The earth for men, Lord Almighty.

Caedmon   Seventh Century

God's Protection

At Tara today in this fateful hour
I place all heaven within its power
And the sun with its brightness
And the snow with its whiteness
And the fire with all the strength it hath,
And lightning with its rapid wrath,
And the winds with their swiftness along their path,
And the sea with its deepness,
And the earth with its starkness:
All these I place,
By God's almighty grace,
Between myself and the powers of darkness.

Attributed to St Patrick

The Shepherd's Eye

Look down O Lord from heaven,
on thy flocks and lambs;
bless their bodies and their souls
and grant that they who have received
thy sign, O Christ, on their foreheads
may be thine own in the day of judgement;
through Jesus Christ our Lord. Amen

Egbert, Archbishop of York   734

Guidance From the Eternal

Eternal light shine in our hearts
Eternal goodness deliver us from evil
Eternal power be our support
Eternal wisdom scatter the darkness
    of our ignorance
Eternal pity have mercy on us
That with all our heart and mind
    and soul and strength we may seek thy face
    and be brought by thine infinite mercy
    to thy holy presence.

Alcuin of York   Eighth Century

As We Get Older

May the right hand of God
Keep us ever in old age,
The grace of Christ
Continually defend us from the enemy.
O Lord direct our hearts in the way of peace;
Through Jesus Christ our Lord. Amen

The Book of Cerne
Bishop Edelwald   Ninth Century

For Our Bishops

Lord Jesus Christ, Thou didst choose Thine apostles
that they might preside over us as teachers;
so also may it please Thee to teach doctrine
to our bishops in the place of Thine apostles,
and to bless and instruct them,
that they may preserve their lives unharmed and
undefiled for ever and ever. Amen

Egbert, Archbishop of York   734

Longings

I wish, O Son of the living God,
O Ancient, Eternal King,
For a little hut in the wilderness,
That it may be my dwelling
A grey lithe lark to be by its side
A clear pool to wash away my sins
Through the grace of the Holy Spirit.
A pleasant church with linen altar cloth,
A dwelling from God of Heaven;
The shining candles above the pure white
   Scriptures . . .
This is the husbandry I would take,
I would choose and will not hide it.

Thoughts attributed to Bishop Colman
as he arrived at Inishboffin   665

Christ be near at either hand,
Christ behind, before me stand,
Christ with me where'er I go,
Christ around, above, below.

Christ be in my heart and mind,
Christ within my soul enshrined,
Christ control my wayward heart,
Christ abide and ne'er depart.

Christ my life and only Way,
Christ my lantern night and day,
Christ be my unchanging friend,
Guide and Shepherd to the end.

after St Patrick
from The People's Mass Book

Peace . . . Peace . . . Peace . . . Pe

Deep peace of the running wave to you
Deep peace of the flowing air to you
Deep peace of the quiet earth to you
Deep peace of the shining stars to you
Deep peace of the Son of peace to you

The Iona Community

E.O.G.—6

From the Book of Deer

Deliver us, O Lord, from evil.
O Lord Jesu Christ, guard ever in all good works.
O fount and author of all good things,
O God empty us from faults,
And replenish us with good virtues.
Through Thee, O Christ Jesu.

From the Book of Dimma

Dearly beloved brethren,
                        Let us pray for our sick brother,
  to Almighty God,
To whom it is easy to restore and establish all his
  good works;
That either in refreshment or renewal the creature
  may feel the hand of the creator; in man of his
  making may the living Father vouchsafe to recreate
  his work.

      I believe in God the Father Almighty
      I believe in Jesus Christ his Son
      And I believe in the Holy Ghost
      I believe in life after death
      I believe in the resurrection

From the Stowe Missal

Thou who guidedst Noah over the flood waves,
Hear us
Who with thy word recalled Jonah from the abyss,
Deliver us
Who stretched forth thy hand to Peter as he sank,
Help us O Christ.
Son of God, thou didst marvellous things of the
    Lord with our Fathers,
Be favourable in our day also;
Stretch forth thy hand from on high.

I implore you, most high God of Sabaoth, Holy Father,
That you would deign to gird me with the tunic of love,
To encompass my loins with the belt of love,
And to burn up the reins of my heart with the fire
    of your love,
So that I may be able to intercede for my sins and
    earn pardon
    for the sins of the people here present,
    and to offer a peace offering for each one;
Me also when with boldness I fall before thee,
Let thou not perish,
    but vouchsafe to wash, adorn and to raise up gently;
Through our Lord.

Thou commandedst peace
Thou gavest peace
Thou didst leave peace.
Give us, O Lord,
Thy peace from heaven and make this
    day peaceful,
And the remaining days of our life do thou
    dispose in thy peace.
Through our Lord.

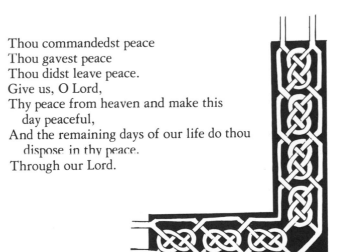

6

ST PATRICK'S BREASTPLATE

The Hymn of St Patrick

I bind unto myself today
The strong name of the Trinity,
By invocation of the same,
The Three in One and One in Three.

I bind this day to me for ever,
By power of faith, Christ's incarnation;
His baptism in the Jordan river;
His death on Cross for my salvation;
His bursting from the spiced tomb;
His riding up the heavenly way;
His coming at the day of doom;
I bind unto myself today . . .

I bind unto myself today
The power of God to hold and lead,
His eye to watch, His might to stay,
His ear to hearken to my need.
The wisdom of my God to teach,
His hand to guide, his shield to ward;
The word of God to give me speech,
His heavenly host to be my guard.

Against all Satan's spells and wiles,
Against false words of heresy,
Against the knowledge that defiles,
Against the heart's idolatry,
Against the wizard's evil craft,
Against the death-wound and the burning,
The choking wave, the poisoned shaft,
Protect me, Christ, till thy returning.

Christ be with me, Christ within me,
Christ behind me, Christ before me,
Christ beside me, Christ to win me,
Christ to comfort and restore me,
Christ beneath me, Christ above me,
Christ in quiet, Christ in danger,
Christ in hearts of all that love me,
Christ in mouth of friend and stranger . . .

tr. C.F. Alexander

The Breastplate of St Patrick

There is no doubt of the faith that St Patrick had in the
saving power of Christ and in his abiding presence.
We can share that same faith by putting on his
'Breastplate'.

CHRIST BE WITH ME

Not a request but a fact; what we seek is an awareness of
this reality. We need to take Him at His word, 'Lo I am
with you always'. Wherever we are, whatever we do,
our God is with us. The Lord is here, his Spirit is with
us.

CHRIST WITHIN ME

There is many a person who has spent his life seeking
Christ and making all sorts of pilgrimages, but the
wonderful message is, 'We dwell in him and he in us'.
If we still ourselves, we will discover he is there. He has
been waiting to work in us and through us. 'In him we
live and move and have our being'.

CHRIST BEHIND ME

There he walks in your past.
He walks in all the dark rooms you pretend are closed,
    that he may bring light.
Invite him into your past. Experience his forgiveness,
    his acceptance of you.
Offer especially all that you are ashamed of
                    all that you wish to forget
                    all that still pains and hurts you
                    all the hurt you have caused others.
Walk there in the places you are afraid of, knowing that
    he walks with you and will lead you on!

CHRIST BEFORE ME

He forever goes before us to prepare a place for us. He is
    on the road we tread. Wherever life is leading us, he
    has gone before. 'Yea, though I walk through the
    valley of the shadow of death, I will fear no evil, for
    thou art with me.' Perhaps we have no clue about
    what lies ahead; we know *who* is ahead of us, so the
    future is not quite unknown.

CHRIST BESIDE ME

The light in the dark.
The presence in our loneliness.
The strength in our weakness.
The guide in our lostness.
He is ready to carry not only our burdens, but us if need
    be.
He *is* the mission that we take to others.

CHRIST TO WIN ME

Let us not belittle the battle — we belong to the Church Militant here on earth. His mission, his salvation, is not yet complete in me. It all has a 'now' and a 'not yet' quality to it. There are many things each day that will shout to hide his voice, that will demand and take away awareness of him. But he remains and, in his love, is still seeking to win me.

CHRIST TO COMFORT AND RESTORE ME

He has come that we should not perish; that our life
    should be everlasting.
He has come that we should have life in all its fullness.
The Comforter, the strengthener.
The Resurrection, the life.
In him I find refreshment, restoration, renewal.
Through him I shall not perish . . . not even today!

CHRIST BENEATH ME

Beneath are the everlasting arms — and they bear the print of the nails. No matter how far I have sunk, he descends to lift me up. He has plumbed all the hells of this world that he may lift us upwards. He is our firm support.

CHRIST ABOVE ME

That at all times he may raise me and lift me up. He became man that he may lift us up to the Godhead. His eye is upon me.
I will not sink, for he lifts me.

CHRIST IN QUIET

In the place of stillness: the room of prayer
In the sanctuary of adoration
In the stilling of the storm
In the stilling of our minds, our souls and bodies
In the peace he gives
In the peace he asks us to share.

CHRIST IN DANGER

In the storm itself
In the sinking of the disciple
In the opposition of the enemy
In the hells and crucifixions
In the betrayals and denials
In the ebbing out of life
The Risen Lord is there.

CHRIST IN HEARTS OF ALL
THAT LOVE ME

Thank God; not only in me but in all who love me.
In them, whether they are aware or not.
My mission is to discover this and reveal it.
Christ comes in love.
When we truly love, we open our life not only to another
but to the great Other who is Christ.
In our sharing together he comes.
Let us release the Christ in each other.

CHRIST IN MOUTH OF FRIEND
AND STRANGER

There is a wonderful way to discover God — in the
    other.
There is an openness and receptiveness in our lives that
    makes room for the Christ.
Our mission is not to bring Christ to others, but to
    discover that he is there and to reveal his presence.
When theology palls and mysticism seems empty there is
    still the third way — our neighbour.

> 'I sought my God,
> My God I could not see.
> I sought my soul,
> My soul eluded me.
> I sought my brother
> And I found all three.'

7

———

THOUGHTS ON HOLY ISLAND

Lord,

There are times when I need to be an island,
Set in an infinite sea
Cut off from all that comes to me
But surrounded still by thee.
Times of quiet and peace
When traffic and turmoil cease
When I can be still and worship thee
Lord of the land and sea.
Full tide and ebb tide
Let life rhythms flow
Ebb tide, full tide
How life's beat must go.

Lord,

I must be part of the mainland,
A causeway between me and others.
There are times when I can only find thee
In working with my brothers.
Times of business and industry
Freeing ourselves from captivity.
It's when we give a helping hand
We meet you, Lord of sea and land.
Ebb tide, full tide
Let life rhythms flow
Full tide, ebb tide
How life's beat must go.

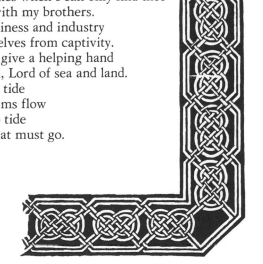